RECORDS ARE IMPORTANT

This improved record book will help you to keep better records of your class and to keep them in one place FOR A WHOLE YEAR!

Records, accurately kept, make a good history of your accomplishments. What a joy at the end of a year's effort to be able to look over the progress you have made in **winning** and **keeping** your class members for the Lord!

VISITING IS IMPORTANT

If your Sunday school increases in quality and attendance in any big and permanent way, you will need to have regular, systematic, carefully planned visitation!

1. VISIT THE REGULAR MEMBERS OF YOUR CLASS. A teacher visits to get better acquainted with the class members as individual persons. Sunday school teaching is guiding persons in their individual Christian growth. This can be done only by an intimate acquaintance with each one in the class.

2. VISIT THE ABSENTEES. Don't let anyone drop out of your Sunday school class! Follow up every Sunday. **Keep the members you have—don't let anyone drop out of your class!**

3. VISIT THE PROSPECTS. Keep a list of prospects for your class. Remember, they are people! Call on them to show your interest and friendship. Keep this up—don't give up—don't stop!

4. HAVE A REGULAR TIME FOR VISITATION. Monday evening is a good time. Why not dedicate one evening each week for service to God and others?

VISITATION SUMMARY FOR THE YEAR

Record here total number of visits teacher makes each week

MONTH	Sept	Oct	N			
1.						
2.						
3.						
4.						
5.						
	QUARTERLY TOTAL			QUARTERLY TOTAL		

MONTH	Mar	Apr	May	Jun	Jul	Aug
1.						
2.						
3.						
4.						
5.						
	QUARTERLY TOTAL			QUARTERLY TOTAL		

ATTENDANCE RECORD FOR YEAR __________

1. Teacher	Birthday
Address	E-mail Address
Phone	Cell Phone
2. Teacher	Birthday
Address	E-mail Address
Phone	Cell Phone
3. Name	Birthday
Address	E-mail Address
Phone	Cell Phone
4. Name	Birthday
Address	E-mail Address
Phone	Cell Phone
5. Name	Birthday
Address	E-mail Address
Phone	Cell Phone
6. Name	Birthday
Address	E-mail Address
Phone	Cell Phone
7. Name	Birthday
Address	E-mail Address
Phone	Cell Phone
8. Name	Birthday
Address	E-mail Address
Phone	Cell Phone

SESSIONS						SESSIONS						SESSIONS						SESSIONS					
	1	2	3	4	5		1	2	3	4	5		1	2	3	4	5		1	2	3	4	5
EPT						DEC						MAR						JUN					
CT						JAN						APR						JUL					
OV						FEB						MAY						AUG					
EPT						DEC						MAR						JUN					
CT						JAN						APR						JUL					
OV						FEB						MAY						AUG					
EPT						DEC						MAR						JUN					
CT						JAN						APR						JUL					
OV						FEB						MAY						AUG					
EPT						DEC						MAR						JUN					
CT						JAN						APR						JUL					
OV						FEB						MAY						AUG					
EPT						DEC						MAR						JUN					
CT						JAN						APR						JUL					
OV						FEB						MAY						AUG					
EPT						DEC						MAR						JUN					
CT						JAN						APR						JUL					
OV						FEB						MAY						AUG					
EPT						DEC						MAR						JUN					
CT						JAN						APR						JUL					
OV						FEB						MAY						AUG					
EPT						DEC						MAR						JUN					
CT						JAN						APR						JUL					
OV						FEB						MAY						AUG					

ATTENDANCE RECORD FOR YEAR __________

9. Name	Birthday
Address	E-mail Address
Phone	Cell Phone
10. Name	Birthday
Address	E-mail Address
Phone	Cell Phone
11. Name	Birthday
Address	E-mail Address
Phone	Cell Phone
12. Name	Birthday
Address	E-mail Address
Phone	Cell Phone
13. Name	Birthday
Address	E-mail Address
Phone	Cell Phone
14. Name	Birthday
Address	E-mail Address
Phone	Cell Phone
15. Name	Birthday
Address	E-mail Address
Phone	Cell Phone
16. Name	Birthday
Address	E-mail Address
Phone	Cell Phone

SESSIONS						SESSIONS						SESSIONS						SESSIONS					
	1	2	3	4	5		1	2	3	4	5		1	2	3	4	5		1	2	3	4	5
PT						DEC						MAR						JUN					
CT						JAN						APR						JUL					
OV						FEB						MAY						AUG					
PT						DEC						MAR						JUN					
CT						JAN						APR						JUL					
OV						FEB						MAY						AUG					
PT						DEC						MAR						JUN					
CT						JAN						APR						JUL					
OV						FEB						MAY						AUG					
EPT						DEC						MAR						JUN					
CT						JAN						APR						JUL					
OV						FEB						MAY						AUG					
EPT						DEC						MAR						JUN					
CT						JAN						APR						JUL					
OV						FEB						MAY						AUG					
EPT						DEC						MAR						JUN					
CT						JAN						APR						JUL					
OV						FEB						MAY						AUG					
EPT						DEC						MAR						JUN					
CT						JAN						APR						JUL					
OV						FEB						MAY						AUG					
EPT						DEC						MAR						JUN					
CT						JAN						APR						JUL					
OV						FEB						MAY						AUG					

ATTENDANCE RECORD FOR YEAR ________

17. Name	Birthday
Address	E-mail Address
Phone	Cell Phone
18. Name	Birthday
Address	E-mail Address
Phone	Cell Phone
19. Name	Birthday
Address	E-mail Address
Phone	Cell Phone
20. Name	Birthday
Address	E-mail Address
Phone	Cell Phone
21. Name	Birthday
Address	E-mail Address
Phone	Cell Phone
22. Name	Birthday
Address	E-mail Address
Phone	Cell Phone
23. Name	Birthday
Address	E-mail Address
Phone	Cell Phone
24. Name	Birthday
Address	E-mail Address
Phone	Cell Phone

SESSIONS						SESSIONS						SESSIONS						SESSIONS					
	1	2	3	4	5		1	2	3	4	5		1	2	3	4	5		1	2	3	4	5
EPT						DEC						MAR						JUN					
CT						JAN						APR						JUL					
OV						FEB						MAY						AUG					
EPT						DEC						MAR						JUN					
CT						JAN						APR						JUL					
OV						FEB						MAY						AUG					
EPT						DEC						MAR						JUN					
CT						JAN						APR						JUL					
OV						FEB						MAY						AUG					
EPT						DEC						MAR						JUN					
CT						JAN						APR						JUL					
OV						FEB						MAY						AUG					
EPT						DEC						MAR						JUN					
CT						JAN						APR						JUL					
OV						FEB						MAY						AUG					
EPT						DEC						MAR						JUN					
CT						JAN						APR						JUL					
OV						FEB						MAY						AUG					
EPT						DEC						MAR						JUN					
CT						JAN						APR						JUL					
OV						FEB						MAY						AUG					
EPT						DEC						MAR						JUN					
CT						JAN						APR						JUL					
OV						FEB						MAY						AUG					

ATTENDANCE SUMMARY FOR THE YEAR

	FALL QUARTER			WINTER QUARTER			SPRING QUARTER			SUMMER QUARTER		
	Students	Visitors	Total	Students	Visitors	Total	Students	Visitors	Total	Students	Visitors	Total
1.												
2.												
3.												
4.												
5.												
6.												
7.												
8.												
9.												
10.												
11.												
12.												
13.												
14.												
Total												

ATTENDANCE TOTAL FOR THE YEAR STUDENTS__________ VISITORS__________ GRAND TOTAL__________

OFFERING SUMMARY FOR THE YEAR

MONTH	Sept	Oct	Nov	Dec	Jan	Feb
1.						
2.						
3.						
4.						
5.						
	QUARTERLY TOTAL			QUARTERLY TOTAL		

MONTH	Mar	Apr	May	Jun	Jul	Aug
1.						
2.						
3.						
4.						
5.						
	QUARTERLY TOTAL			QUARTERLY TOTAL		